AL QUR'AN TRACING WORKBOOK

HOW TO MASTER 14 SHORT SURAHS AND AYATUL KURSI WITH WORD-BY-WORD UNDERSTANDING IN ENGLISH

BLACK AND WHITE EDITION

TRACE AND MEMORISE

Name:	Starting Date:

Compiled by:
Rahmi Kurnia

Copyright © Rahmi Kurnia

All rights reserved. No part of this book may be used or reproduced by any means, graphic, electronic, or mechanical, including photocopying, recording, taping, or by any information storage retrieval system without the written permission of the publisher except in the case of brief quotations embodied in critical articles and reviews.

Compiled by
Rahmi Kurnia

Cover Design by
Rahmi Kurnia & Musa Ibrahim

Published by
Arke Books

A catalogue record for this book is available from the British Library.

ISBN: 978-1-0685880-6-8

Special thanks to my family who helped me so much in completing this book, may Allāh bless them all.

More books from arkebooks:

CONTENTS

Steps to Memorise the Surahs Effectively 4
How to Use this Book 5
Surah Al-Fātihah (1) 7
Surah An-Nās (2) 16
Surah Al-Falaq (3) 22
Surah Al-Ikhlās (4) 28
Surah Al-Masad (5) 33
Surah An-Nasr (6) 39
Surah Al-Kāfirūn (7) 44
Surah Al-Kawthar (8) 50
Surah Al-Mā'un (9) 55
Surah Quraysh (10) 63
Surah Al-Fīl (11) 68
Surah Al-Humazah (12) 74
Surah Al-'Asr (13) 83
Surah At-Takāthur (14) 88
Ayatul Kursi 96
My Surah Tracker 104

STEPS TO MEMORISE THE SURAHS EFFECTIVELY

1. Make the Right Intention in Your Heart
   − Have a sincere intention to memorise the Surah only to please Allah.

2. Ask Allah for Ease and Guidance
   − Begin with a du'a, asking Allah to make the memorisation process easy for you.

3. Understand the Meaning of Each Verse
   − Learn the meaning of each verse word by word to strengthen both memorisation and understanding.

4. Memorise One Verse at a Time
   − Repeat the verse several times until you've fully memorised it.
   − Do not move on to the next verse until you have mastered the current one.
   − Recite aloud while memorising.

5. Connect the Verses Together
   − After memorising a new verse, recite it together with the previous one to build fluency and connection.

6. Continue Until You Finish the Surah
   − Repeat steps 4 and 5 until you reach the last verse of the surah.

7. Revise the Entire Surah
   − Review the whole surah regularly until it is firmly memorised. Only then move on to the next surah.

8. Recite the Memorised Surah in Your Salah
   − Use what you've memorised in your daily prayers to reinforce it.

9. Listen to a Qari' for Correct Pronunciation
   − Choose your favorite Qari' (reciter) and listen to them often to improve your tajweed and pronunciation.

May Allah make your memorisation journey easy, blessed, and full of barakah.

Keep going, one verse at a time!

HOW TO USE THIS BOOK

1. Trace the Arabic words and transliterations (remember to write Arabic from right to left).

2. Write the Arabic words by yourself to reinforce your handwriting and memory.

3. Trace the English meanings to understand the vocabulary.

4. Read each word aloud while you trace and write it.

Read

A. TRACE AND READ | **Full Surah**

بِسْمِ ٱللَّهِ ٱلرَّحْمَـٰنِ ٱلرَّحِيمِ ﴿١﴾

Trace

بِسْمِ ٱللَّهِ ٱلرَّحْمَـٰنِ ٱلرَّحِيمِ

Trace → Bismillāhir Rahmānir Rahīm

In the name of Allāh, the Entirely Merciful, the Especially Merciful.

Trace

B. TRACE AND WRITE | **Word by Word**

Trace

﴿١﴾ ٱلرَّحِيمِ ٱلرَّحْمَـٰنِ ٱللَّهِ بِسْمِ

al rahīmi | al rahmāni | al lāhi | Bismi

Write

بِسْمِ

the Most Merciful. | the Most Gracious, | (of) Allāh | In (the) name

C. TRACE AND TRANSLATE | **Word by Word**

Translate the following:

Trace

ٱلرَّحِيمِ ٱلرَّحْمَـٰنِ ٱللَّهِ بِسْمِ

			In (the) name

Translate

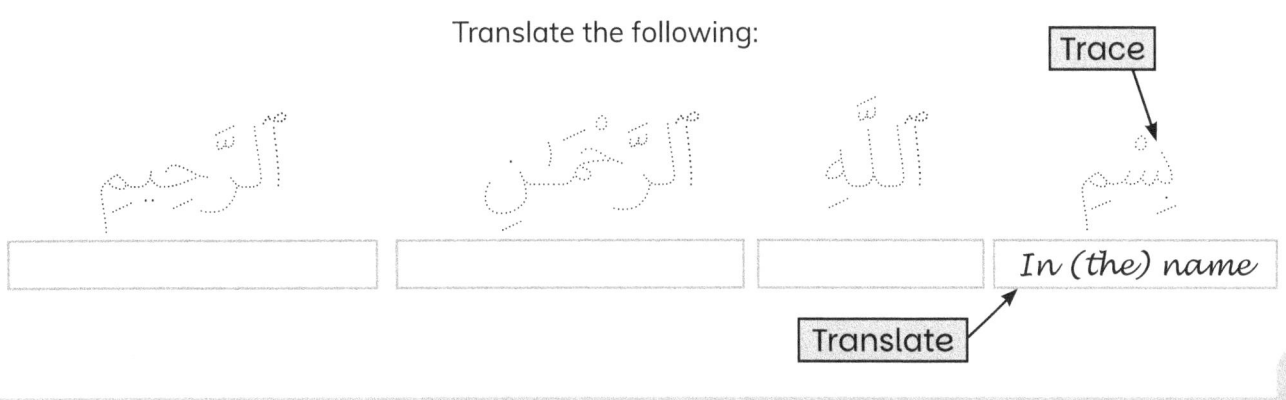

5. Match Arabic words to their English meanings to build comprehension.

D. MATCH THE PAIRS

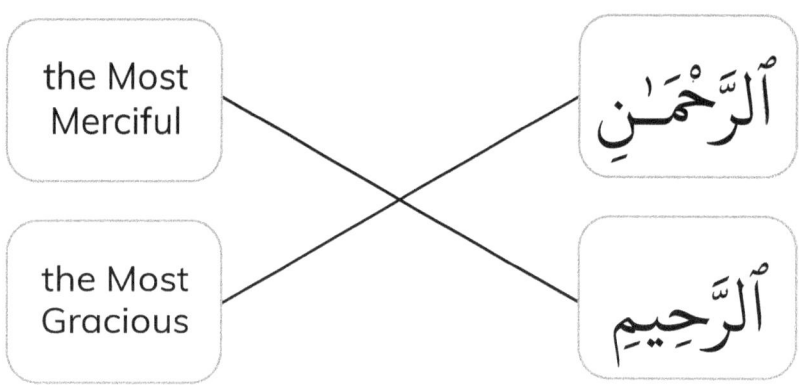

6. Memorise the verses one at a time for steady progress (master each verse before moving on).

E. TRACE AND MEMORISE | Memorisation

Memorise one verse at a time.

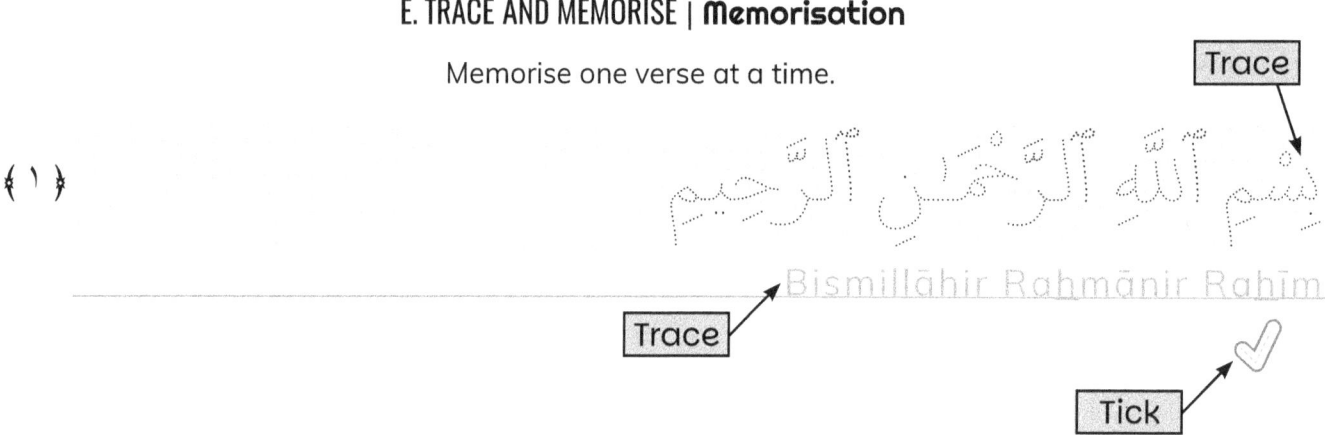

Tick it once you've memorised this verse.
Do not move on to the next verse until you've mastered this one.

7. Record your memorisation on the **My Surah Tracker** page to track your achievement.

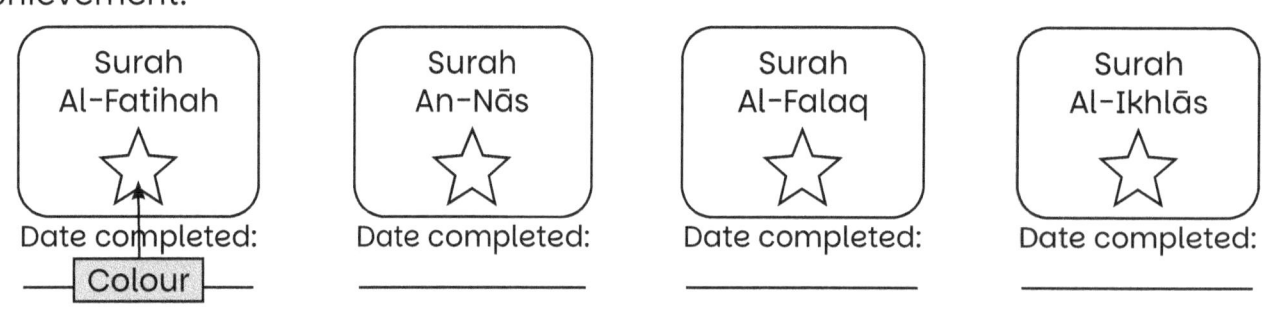

8. Scan the **QR** code on page 104 to access the answer key.

9. **Meccan**/Makki Surahs, revealed in Makkah before the Hijrah, focus on faith, Tawheed, and the Hereafter, while **Medinan**/Madani Surahs, revealed in Madinah after the Hijrah, focus on laws, social issues, and community life.

10. In Arabic transliteration, the long vowels are written as **ā** or **aa** for long alif (ا), **ī** or **ee** or **ii** for long yā' (ي), and **ū** or **oo** or **uu** for long wāw (و) to clearly distinguish them from short vowels a, i, u.

Translation by: Saheeh International

Juz 1 | Surah 1 | Meccan

Surah Al-Fātihah | The Opening
7 Ayahs/Verses
TRACE AND READ | Full Surah

Date:_____

Part 1

1A

بِسْمِ ٱللَّهِ ٱلرَّحْمَٰنِ ٱلرَّحِيمِ ﴿١﴾

Bismillāhir Rahmānir Rahīm
In the name of Allāh, the Entirely Merciful, the Especially Merciful.

ٱلْحَمْدُ لِلَّهِ رَبِّ ٱلْعَٰلَمِينَ ﴿٢﴾

Alhamdu lillāhi Rabbil 'ālamīn
[All] praise is [due] to Allāh, Lord of the worlds

ٱلرَّحْمَٰنِ ٱلرَّحِيمِ ﴿٣﴾

Ar Rahmānir Rahīm
The Entirely Merciful, the Especially Merciful,

مَٰلِكِ يَوْمِ ٱلدِّينِ ﴿٤﴾

Māliki Yawmid Dīn
Sovereign of the Day of Recompense.

إِيَّاكَ نَعْبُدُ وَإِيَّاكَ نَسْتَعِينُ ﴿٥﴾

'Iyyāka na'budu wa 'iyyāka nasta'īn
It is You we worship and You we ask for help.

اهْدِنَا الصِّرَاطَ الْمُسْتَقِيمَ ﴿٦﴾

'Ihdinas sirātal Mustaqīm
Guide us to the straight path

صِرَاطَ الَّذِينَ أَنْعَمْتَ عَلَيْهِمْ غَيْرِ الْمَغْضُوبِ عَلَيْهِمْ وَلَا الضَّالِّينَ ﴿٧﴾

sirātalladhīna 'an'amta 'alayhim
ghayril maghdūbi 'alayhim wa lad dāllīn

The path of those upon whom You have bestowed favor, not of those who have earned [Your] anger or of those who are astray.

Surah Al-Fātihah | The Opening
7 Ayahs/Verses

Juz 1 / Surah 1 — Meccan

TRACE AND WRITE | Word by Word

Part 1 — 1B

Date: _____

(1) بِسْمِ ٱللَّٰهِ ٱلرَّحْمَٰنِ ٱلرَّحِيمِ

al raḥīmi   al raḥmāni   al lāhi   Bismi

the Most Merciful,   the Most Gracious,   (of) Allāh   In (the) name

(2) ٱلْحَمْدُ لِلَّٰهِ رَبِّ ٱلْعَٰلَمِينَ

al 'ālamīna   rabbi   lillāhi   Alḥamdu

(of all) the worlds   the Lord   (be) to Allāh   All praises and thanks

(3) ٱلرَّحْمَٰنِ ٱلرَّحِيمِ

al raḥīmi   al raḥmāni

the Most Merciful,   The Most Gracious,

(4) مَٰلِكِ يَوْمِ ٱلدِّينِ

al dīni   yawmi   Māliki

(of the) Judgement   (of the) Day   (The) Master

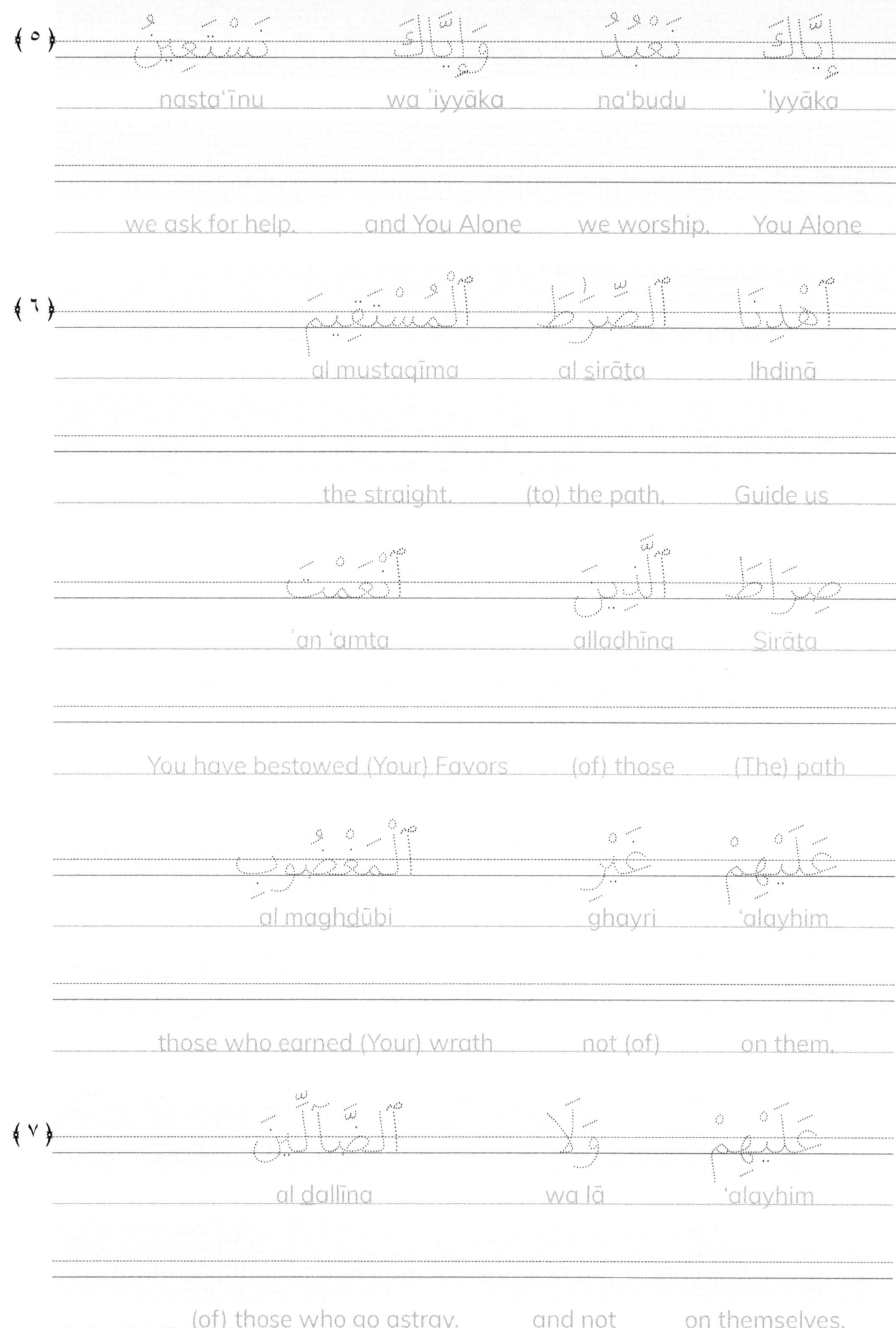

Surah Al-Fātihah | The Opening
7 Ayahs/Verses

Juz 1 / Surah 1 / Meccan

Date:_____

TRACE AND TRANSLATE | Word by Word

Part 1

Translate the following:

1C

ٱلرَّحِيمِ   ٱلرَّحْمَٰنِ   ٱللَّهِ   بِسْمِ

ٱلْعَٰلَمِينَ   رَبِّ   لِلَّهِ   ٱلْحَمْدُ

ٱلرَّحِيمِ   ٱلرَّحْمَٰنِ

ٱلدِّينِ   يَوْمِ   مَٰلِكِ

نَسْتَعِينُ   وَإِيَّاكَ   نَعْبُدُ   إِيَّاكَ

ٱلْمُسْتَقِيمَ   ٱلصِّرَٰطَ   ٱهْدِنَا

11

صِرَاطَ   ٱلَّذِينَ   أَنْعَمْتَ

عَلَيْهِمْ   غَيْرِ   ٱلْمَغْضُوبِ

عَلَيْهِمْ   وَلَا   ٱلضَّالِّينَ

Surah Al-Fātihah | The Opening
7 Ayahs/Verses
MATCH THE PAIRS

Part 1

the Most Merciful	ٱلرَّحْمَٰنِ
(the) Master	ٱلرَّحِيمِ
the Judgement	مَٰلِكِ
the straight	صِرَاطَ
in (the) name	ٱلْمُسْتَقِيمَ
the Most Gracious	ٱلدِّينِ
(the) path	بِسْمِ

Surah Al-Fātihah | The Opening
7 Ayahs/Verses

TRACE AND MEMORISE | Memorisation

Date completed: _____

Part 1

Memorise one verse at a time.

1E

﴿١﴾ بِسْمِ اللَّهِ الرَّحْمَٰنِ الرَّحِيمِ

Bismillāhir Rahmānir Rahīm

﴿٢﴾ الْحَمْدُ لِلَّهِ رَبِّ الْعَالَمِينَ

Alhamdu lillāhi Rabbil 'ālamīn

﴿٣﴾ الرَّحْمَٰنِ الرَّحِيمِ

Ar Rahmānir Rahīm

﴿٤﴾ مَالِكِ يَوْمِ الدِّينِ

Māliki Yawmid Dīn

﴿٥﴾ إِيَّاكَ نَعْبُدُ وَإِيَّاكَ نَسْتَعِينُ

'Iyyāka na'budu wa 'iyyāka nasta'īn

﴿٦﴾ اهْدِنَا الصِّرَاطَ الْمُسْتَقِيمَ

Ihdinaṣ ṣirāṭal Mustaqīm

صِرَاطَ ٱلَّذِينَ أَنْعَمْتَ عَلَيْهِمْ
sirātalladhīna 'an'amta 'alayhim

⟨٧⟩ غَيْرِ ٱلْمَغْضُوبِ عَلَيْهِمْ وَلَا ٱلضَّآلِّينَ
ghayril maghdūbi 'alayhim wa lad dāllīn

| Juz 30, Surah 114 | Meccan |

Surah An-Nās | The Mankind
6 Ayahs/Verses

TRACE AND READ | Full Surah

Date:_____

Part 2

بِسْمِ ٱللَّهِ ٱلرَّحْمَٰنِ ٱلرَّحِيمِ

قُلْ أَعُوذُ بِرَبِّ ٱلنَّاسِ ﴿١﴾

Qul 'a'ūdhu birabbin nās
Say, "I seek refuge in the Lord of mankind,

مَلِكِ ٱلنَّاسِ ﴿٢﴾

Malikin nās
The Sovereign of mankind,

إِلَٰهِ ٱلنَّاسِ ﴿٣﴾

'Ilāhin nās
The God of mankind,

مِن شَرِّ ٱلْوَسْوَاسِ ٱلْخَنَّاسِ ﴿٤﴾

Min sharril was wāsil khannās
From the evil of the retreating whisperer

Surah An-Nās | The Mankind
6 Ayahs/Verses

Juz 30 / Surah 114 / Meccan

Part 2 — **2B**

Date:_____

TRACE AND WRITE | Word by Word

بِسْمِ ٱللَّهِ ٱلرَّحْمَٰنِ ٱلرَّحِيمِ

﴿١﴾ قُلْ أَعُوذُ بِرَبِّ ٱلنَّاسِ

Qul	'a'ūdhu	birabbi	al nāsi
Say,	I seek refuge	in (the) Lord	(of) mankind.

ٱلَّذِى يُوَسْوِسُ فِى صُدُورِ ٱلنَّاسِ ﴿٥﴾

Alladhī yuwaswisu fī sudūrin nās
Who whispers [evil] into the breasts of mankind

مِنَ ٱلْجِنَّةِ وَٱلنَّاسِ ﴿٦﴾

Minal jinnati wan nās
From among the jinn and mankind".

17

(٢) مَلِكِ ٱلنَّاسِ

Maliki   al nāsi

(The) King   (of) mankind.

(٣) إِلَٰهِ ٱلنَّاسِ

'Ilāhi   al nāsi

(The) God   (of) mankind.

(٤) مِن شَرِّ ٱلْوَسْوَاسِ ٱلْخَنَّاسِ

Min   sharri   al waswāsi   al khannāsi

From   (the) evil   (of) the whisperer   the one who withdraws

(٥) ٱلَّذِي يُوَسْوِسُ فِي صُدُورِ ٱلنَّاسِ

'Alladhī   yuwaswisu   fī   sudūri   al nāsi

The one who   whispers   in   (the) breasts   (of) mankind.

(٦) مِنَ ٱلْجِنَّةِ وَٱلنَّاسِ

Mina   al jinnati   wal nāsi

From   the jinn   and men.

Surah An-Nās | The Mankind
6 Ayahs/Verses

Juz 30 | Surah 114 | Meccan

TRACE AND TRANSLATE | Word by Word

Date:_____

Part 2 — Translate the following: — 2C

ٱلنَّاسِ	بِرَبِّ	أَعُوذُ	قُلْ
☐	☐	☐	☐

ٱلنَّاسِ	مَلِكِ
☐	☐

ٱلنَّاسِ	إِلَٰهِ
☐	☐

ٱلْخَنَّاسِ	ٱلْوَسْوَاسِ	شَرِّ	مِن
☐	☐	☐	☐

ٱلنَّاسِ	صُدُورِ	فِي	يُوَسْوِسُ	ٱلَّذِي
☐	☐	☐	☐	☐

وَٱلنَّاسِ	ٱلْجِنَّةِ	مِنَ
☐	☐	☐

Surah An-Nās | The Mankind
6 Ayahs/Verses
MATCH THE PAIRS

Juz 30 / Surah 114 — Meccan

Part 2 — 2D

Date:_____

the jinn	قُلْ
say	مَلِكِ
(of) mankind	ٱلنَّاسِ
(the) King	ٱلْجِنَّةِ
from	مِنَ
in	فِي

Surah An-Nās | The Mankind
6 Ayahs/Verses

Juz 30 | Surah 114 | Meccan

TRACE AND MEMORISE | Memorisation

Date completed: _____

Part 2 — 2E

Memorise one verse at a time.

بِسْمِ ٱللَّهِ ٱلرَّحْمَٰنِ ٱلرَّحِيمِ

﴿١﴾ قُلْ أَعُوذُ بِرَبِّ ٱلنَّاسِ

Qul 'a'ūdhu birabbin nās

✓

﴿٢﴾ مَلِكِ ٱلنَّاسِ

Malikin nās

✓

﴿٣﴾ إِلَٰهِ ٱلنَّاسِ

'Ilāhin nās

✓

﴿٤﴾ مِن شَرِّ ٱلْوَسْوَاسِ ٱلْخَنَّاسِ

Min sharril was wāsil khannās

✓

﴿٥﴾ ٱلَّذِي يُوَسْوِسُ فِي صُدُورِ ٱلنَّاسِ

Alladhī yuwaswisu fī sudūrin nās

✓

﴿٦﴾ مِنَ ٱلْجِنَّةِ وَٱلنَّاسِ

Minal jinnati wan nās

Surah Al-Falaq | The Dawn

Juz 30 · Surah 113 · Meccan
5 Ayahs/Verses

TRACE AND READ | Full Surah

Date:_____

Part 3 — 3A

بِسْمِ ٱللَّهِ ٱلرَّحْمَٰنِ ٱلرَّحِيمِ

قُلْ أَعُوذُ بِرَبِّ ٱلْفَلَقِ ﴿١﴾

Qul 'a'ūdhu bi rabbil falaq
Say, "I seek refuge in the Lord of daybreak

مِن شَرِّ مَا خَلَقَ ﴿٢﴾

Min sharri mā khalaq
From the evil of that which He created

وَمِن شَرِّ غَاسِقٍ إِذَا وَقَبَ ﴿٣﴾

Wa min sharri ghāsiqin 'idhā waqab
And from the evil of darkness when it settles

وَمِن شَرِّ ٱلنَّفَّاثَاتِ فِي ٱلْعُقَدِ ﴿٤﴾

Wa min sharrin naffā thāti fil 'uqad
And from the evil of the blowers in knots

وَمِن شَرِّ حَاسِدٍ إِذَا حَسَدَ ﴿٥﴾

وَمِن شَرِّ حَاسِدٍ إِذَا حَسَدَ

Wa min sharri hāsidin 'idhā hasad
And from the evil of an envier when he envies."

| Juz 30 Surah 113 | Meccan |

Surah Al-Falaq | The Dawn
5 Ayahs/Verses
TRACE AND WRITE | Word by Word

Date:_____

Part 3

3B

بِسْمِ اللَّهِ الرَّحْمَٰنِ الرَّحِيمِ

﴿١﴾ الْفَلَقِ / birabbi / a'ūdhu / Qul

(of) the dawn / in (the) Lord / I seek refuge / Say,

﴿٢﴾ khalaqa / mā / sharri / Min

He created. / (of) what / (the) evil / From

﴿٣﴾ waqaba / 'idhā / ghāsiqin / sharri / Wa min

it settles. / when / (of) darkness / (the) evil / And from

23

{4} وَمِن شَرِّ ٱلنَّفَّاثَاتِ فِي ٱلْعُقَدِ

Wa min　　sharri　　al naffāthāti　　fī　　al 'uqadi

And from　(the) evil　(of) the blowers　in　the knots.

{5} وَمِن شَرِّ حَاسِدٍ إِذَا حَسَدَ

Wa min　　sharri　　ḥāsidin　　'idhā　　ḥasada

And from　(the) evil　(of) an envier　when　he envies.

| Juz 30 Surah 113 | Meccan |

Surah Al-Falaq | The Dawn
5 Ayahs/Verses
TRACE AND TRANSLATE | Word by Word

Date:_____

Part 3

Translate the following:

3C

اَلْفَلَقِ رَبِّ أَعُوذُ قُلْ

☐ ☐ ☐ ☐

خَلَقَ مَا شَرِّ مِنْ

☐ ☐ ☐ ☐

وَقَبَ إِذَا غَاسِقٍ شَرِّ وَمِنْ

☐ ☐ ☐ ☐ ☐

الْعُقَدِ فِي النَّفَّاثَاتِ شَرِّ وَمِنْ

☐ ☐ ☐ ☐ ☐

حَسَدَ إِذَا حَاسِدٍ شَرِّ وَمِنْ

☐ ☐ ☐ ☐ ☐

Surah Al-Falaq | The Dawn
5 Ayahs/Verses

MATCH THE PAIRS

Juz 30 | Surah 113 | Meccan

Date:_____

Part 3 — 3D

(of) the dawn	قُلْ
say	ٱلْفَلَقِ
the knots	مَا
when	ٱلْعُقَدِ
(of) what	إِذَا
(the) darkness	شَرِّ
(the) evil	غَاسِقٍ

| Juz 30 Surah 113 | Meccan |

Surah Al-Falaq | The Dawn
5 Ayahs/Verses

TRACE AND MEMORISE | **Memorisation**

Part 3

Date completed: _____

3E

Memorise one verse at a time.

بِسْمِ ٱللَّهِ ٱلرَّحْمَٰنِ ٱلرَّحِيمِ

﴿١﴾ قُلْ أَعُوذُ بِرَبِّ ٱلْفَلَقِ
Qul 'a'ūdhu bi rabbil falaq ✓

﴿٢﴾ مِن شَرِّ مَا خَلَقَ
Min sharri mā khalaq ✓

﴿٣﴾ وَمِن شَرِّ غَاسِقٍ إِذَا وَقَبَ
Wa min sharri ghāsiqin 'idhā waqab ✓

﴿٤﴾ وَمِن شَرِّ ٱلنَّفَّٰثَٰتِ فِى ٱلْعُقَدِ
Wa min sharrin-naffā-thāti fil 'uqad ✓

﴿٥﴾ وَمِن شَرِّ حَاسِدٍ إِذَا حَسَدَ
Wa min sharri hāsidin 'idhā hasad ✓

| Juz 30 Surah 112 | Meccan |

Surah Al-Ikhlās | Sincerity
4 Ayahs/Verses
TRACE AND READ | Full Surah

Date:_____

Part 4

4A

بِسْمِ ٱللَّهِ ٱلرَّحْمَٰنِ ٱلرَّحِيمِ

قُلْ هُوَ ٱللَّهُ أَحَدٌ ﴿١﴾

Qul huwal lāhu 'ahad
Say, "He is Allāh, [who is] One,

ٱللَّهُ ٱلصَّمَدُ ﴿٢﴾

Allāhus samad
Allāh, the Eternal Refuge.

لَمْ يَلِدْ وَلَمْ يُولَدْ ﴿٣﴾

Lam yalid wa lam yūlad
He neither begets nor is born,

وَلَمْ يَكُن لَّهُ كُفُوًا أَحَدٌ ﴿٤﴾

Wa lam yakul lahū kufuwan 'ahad
Nor is there to Him any equivalent."

Juz 30	
Surah 112	Meccan

Surah Al-Ikhlās | Sincerity
4 Ayahs/Verses
TRACE AND WRITE | Word by Word

Date:_____

Part 4

4B

بِسْمِ ٱللَّهِ ٱلرَّحْمَٰنِ ٱلرَّحِيمِ

(١) أَحَدٌ ٱللَّهُ هُوَ قُلْ

'aḥadun · al lāhu · huwa · Qul

(the) One. · (is) Allāh · He · Say,

(٢) ٱللَّهُ ٱلصَّمَدُ

al ṣamadu · Al lāhu

the Eternal, the Absolute. · Allāh

(٣) لَمْ يَلِدْ وَلَمْ يُولَدْ

yūlad · walam · yalid · Lam

He is begotten. · and not · He begets · Not

(٤) وَلَمْ يَكُن لَّهُ كُفُوًا أَحَدٌ

'aḥadun · kufuwan · lahū · yakun · Walam

any (one) · equivalent · for Him · is · And not

29

Surah Al-Ikhlās | Sincerity
4 Ayahs/Verses

TRACE AND TRANSLATE | Word by Word

Juz 30 · Surah 112 · Meccan

Part 4 — 4C

Date:_____

Translate the following:

أَحَدٌ   ٱللَّهُ   هُوَ   قُلْ
____   ____   ____   ____

ٱللَّهُ   ٱلصَّمَدُ
____   ____

يُولَدْ   وَلَمْ   يَلِدْ   لَمْ
____   ____   ____   ____

أَحَدٌۢ   كُفُوًا   لَّهُۥ   يَكُن   وَلَمْ
____   ____   ____   ____   ____

Surah Al-Ikhlās | Sincerity
4 Ayahs/Verses
MATCH THE PAIRS

Juz 30 Surah 112 — Meccan

Part 4 — 4D

Date:_____

the Eternal, the Absolute	لَمْ
not	ٱلصَّمَدُ
say	يَلِدْ
for Him	هُوَ
He begets	كُفُوًا
He	قُلْ
equivalent	لَّهُۥ

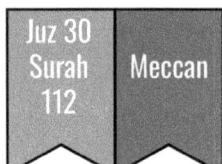

Surah Al-Ikhlās | Sincerity
4 Ayahs/Verses

TRACE AND MEMORISE | Memorisation

Part 4

Date completed: _____

4E

Memorise one verse at a time.

{١} Qul huwal lāhu 'ahad

{٢} Allāhus samad

{٣} Lam yalid wa lam yūlad

{٤} Wa lam yakul lahū kufuwan 'ahad

32 | Part 4

Juz 30 | Surah 111 | Meccan

Surah Al-Masad | The Palm Fibre
5 Ayahs/Verses

TRACE AND READ | Full Surah

Date:_____

Part 5

5A

بِسْمِ ٱللَّهِ ٱلرَّحْمَٰنِ ٱلرَّحِيمِ

تَبَّتْ يَدَآ أَبِى لَهَبٍ وَتَبَّ ﴿١﴾

Tabbat yadā 'abī Lahabiw wa tabb
May the hands of Abū Lahab be ruined, and ruined is he.

مَآ أَغْنَىٰ عَنْهُ مَالُهُۥ وَمَا كَسَبَ ﴿٢﴾

Mā 'aghnā 'anhu māluhū wa mā kasab
His wealth will not avail him or that which he gained.

سَيَصْلَىٰ نَارًا ذَاتَ لَهَبٍ ﴿٣﴾

Sa yaslā nāran dhāta lahab
He will [enter to] burn in a Fire of [blazing] flame

وَٱمْرَأَتُهُۥ حَمَّالَةَ ٱلْحَطَبِ ﴿٤﴾

Wam ra 'atuhū hamma latal hatab
And his wife [as well] - the carrier of firewood.

فِى جِيدِهَا حَبْلٌ مِّن مَّسَدٍ ﴿٥﴾

Fī jīdihā ḥab lum mim masad

Around her neck is a rope of [twisted] fiber.

Juz 30 Surah 111	Meccan

Surah Al-Masad | The Palm Fibre
5 Ayahs/Verses
TRACE AND WRITE | Word by Word

Date: _____

Part 5 | 5B

بِسْمِ ٱللَّهِ ٱلرَّحْمَٰنِ ٱلرَّحِيمِ

﴿١﴾ وَتَبَّ   لَهَبٍ   أَبِى   يَدَا   تَبَّتْ

watabba   lahabin   'abī   yadā   Tabbat

and perish he.   Lahab   (of) Abu   (the) hands   Perish

﴿٢﴾ كَسَبَ   وَمَا   مَالُهُۥ   عَنْهُ   أَغْنَىٰ   مَآ

kasaba   wa mā   māluhū   'anhu   'aghnā   Mā

he earned.   and what   his wealth   him   (will) avail   Not

﴿٣﴾ لَهَبٍ   ذَاتَ   نَارًا   سَيَصْلَىٰ

lahabin   dhāta   nāran   Sayaṣlā

Blazing Flames.   of   (in) a Fire   He will be burnt

(٤) وَامْرَأَتُهُ حَمَّالَةَ الْحَطَبِ

                              al ḥaṭabi   ḥammālata   Wamra'atuhū

                             (of) firewood.   (the) carrier   And his wife

(٥) فِي جِيدِهَا حَبْلٌ مِنْ مَسَدٍ

                       masadin   min   ḥablun   jīdihā   Fī

                       palm-fiber   of   (will be) a rope   her neck   In

Surah Al-Masad | The Palm Fibre
5 Ayahs/Verses

Juz 30 | Surah 111 | Meccan

TRACE AND TRANSLATE | Word by Word

Date:_____

Part 5 — 5C

Translate the following:

وَتَبَّ	أَبِي لَهَبٍ	يَدَا	تَبَّتْ
☐	☐	☐	☐

كَسَبَ	وَمَا	مَالُهُ	عَنْهُ	أَغْنَىٰ	مَا
☐	☐	☐	☐	☐	☐

ذَاتَ لَهَبٍ	نَارًا	سَيَصْلَىٰ
☐	☐	☐

الْحَطَبِ	حَمَّالَةَ	وَامْرَأَتُهُ
☐	☐	☐

مَسَدٍ	مِنْ	حَبْلٌ	جِيدِهَا	فِي
☐	☐	☐	☐	☐

Surah Al-Masad | The Palm Fibre
5 Ayahs/Verses
MATCH THE PAIRS

Juz 30 | Surah 111 | Meccan

Part 5 — 5D

and what	مَّسَدٍ
his wealth	أَبِى لَهَبٍ
(of) Abu Lahab	وَمَا
(in) a Fire	تَبَّتْ
palm-fibre	مَالُهُۥ
(of) firewood	نَارًا
perish	ٱلْحَطَبِ

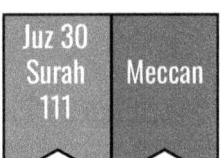

Surah Al-Masad | The Palm Fibre
5 Ayahs/Verses
TRACE AND MEMORISE | Memorisation

Date completed: _____

Part 5

Memorise one verse at a time.

بِسْمِ ٱللَّهِ ٱلرَّحْمَٰنِ ٱلرَّحِيمِ

﴿١﴾ تَبَّتْ يَدَآ أَبِي لَهَبٍ وَتَبَّ

Tabbat yadā 'abī Lahabiw wa tabb

﴿٢﴾ مَآ أَغْنَىٰ عَنْهُ مَالُهُۥ وَمَا كَسَبَ

Mā 'aghnā 'anhu māluhū wa mā kasab

﴿٣﴾ سَيَصْلَىٰ نَارًا ذَاتَ لَهَبٍ

Sa yas lā nāran dhāta lahab

﴿٤﴾ وَٱمْرَأَتُهُۥ حَمَّالَةَ ٱلْحَطَبِ

Wam ra 'atuhū hamma latal hatab

﴿٥﴾ فِي جِيدِهَا حَبْلٌ مِّن مَّسَدٍۭ

Fī jīdihā hab lum mim masad

Juz 30 | Surah 110 | Medinan

Surah An-Nasr | Divine Support
3 Ayahs/Verses

TRACE AND READ | Full Surah

Date:_____

Part 6

6A

بِسْمِ ٱللَّهِ ٱلرَّحْمَٰنِ ٱلرَّحِيمِ

إِذَا جَآءَ نَصْرُ ٱللَّهِ وَٱلْفَتْحُ ﴿١﴾

'Idhā jā 'a nasrullāhi walfath

When the victory of Allāh has come and the conquest,

وَرَأَيْتَ ٱلنَّاسَ يَدْخُلُونَ فِي دِينِ ٱللَّهِ أَفْوَاجًا ﴿٢﴾

Wa ra 'aytan nāsa yadkhulūna fī dīnillāhi 'afwājā

And you see the people entering into the religion of Allāh in multitudes,

فَسَبِّحْ بِحَمْدِ رَبِّكَ وَٱسْتَغْفِرْهُ ۚ إِنَّهُۥ كَانَ تَوَّابًا ﴿٣﴾

Fa sabbih bihamdi rabbika wastaghfirh.'Innahū kāna tawwābā

Then exalt [Him] with praise of your Lord and ask forgiveness of Him. Indeed, He is ever Accepting of Repentance.

Surah An-Nasr | Divine Support
3 Ayahs/Verses

Juz 30 | Surah 110 | Medinan

Part 6 — 6B

TRACE AND WRITE | Word by Word

Date:_____

بِسْمِ اللَّهِ الرَّحْمَٰنِ الرَّحِيمِ

{1}

wal fathu	al lāhi	naṣru	jā'a	'Idhā
and the Victory.	(of) Allāh	(the) Help	comes	When

fī	yadkhulūna	al nāsa	Wara'ayta
into	entering	the people	And you see

{2}

'afwājan	al lāhi	dīni
(in) multitudes.	(of) Allāh	(the) religion

wa istaghfirhu	rabbika	bihamdi	Fasabbiḥ
and ask His forgiveness.	(of) your Lord	with (the) praises	The glorify

(٣) _____ إِنَّهُۥ كَانَ تَوَّابًۢا

tawwāban   kāna   'Innahū

Oft-Returning.   is   Indeed, He

Juz 30 | Surah 110 | Medinan

Surah An-Nasr | Divine Support
3 Ayahs/Verses

TRACE AND TRANSLATE | Word by Word

Part 6

Date: _____

6C

Translate the following:

إِذَا   جَآءَ   نَصْرُ   ٱللَّهِ   وَٱلْفَتْحُ

وَرَأَيْتَ   ٱلنَّاسَ   يَدْخُلُونَ   فِى

دِينِ   ٱللَّهِ   أَفْوَاجًا

فَسَبِّحْ   بِحَمْدِ   رَبِّكَ   وَٱسْتَغْفِرْهُ

إِنَّهُۥ   كَانَ   تَوَّابًۢا

41

Surah An-Nasr | Divine Support
3 Ayahs/Verses
MATCH THE PAIRS

Part 6

the glorify	رَبِّكَ
into	فَسَبِّحْ
(the) praises	فِى
(of) your Lord	دِينِ
and the Victory	نَصْرُ
(the) religion	وَٱلْفَتْحُ
(the) Help	بِحَمْدِ

Surah An-Nasr | Divine Support
3 Ayahs/Verses
TRACE AND MEMORISE | Memorisation

Juz 30 | Surah 110 | Medinan

Part 6 — 6E

Memorise one verse at a time.

بِسْمِ ٱللَّهِ ٱلرَّحْمَٰنِ ٱلرَّحِيمِ

{١} إِذَا جَآءَ نَصْرُ ٱللَّهِ وَٱلْفَتْحُ

'Idhā jā 'a naṣ rullāhi walfath ✓

{٢} وَرَأَيْتَ ٱلنَّاسَ يَدْخُلُونَ فِي دِينِ ٱللَّهِ أَفْوَاجًا

Wa ra 'aytan nāsa yadkhulūna fī dīnillāhi 'afwājā ✓

{٣} فَسَبِّحْ بِحَمْدِ رَبِّكَ وَٱسْتَغْفِرْهُ ۚ إِنَّهُ كَانَ تَوَّابًا

Fa sabbiḥ biḥamdi rabbika wastaghfirh. 'Innahū kāna tawwābā ✓

Surah Al-Kāfirūn | The Disbelievers
6 Ayahs/Verses

Juz 30 | Surah 109 | Meccan

TRACE AND READ | Full Surah

Part 7

بِسْمِ ٱللَّهِ ٱلرَّحْمَٰنِ ٱلرَّحِيمِ

قُلْ يَٰٓأَيُّهَا ٱلْكَٰفِرُونَ ﴿١﴾

Qul yā 'ayyuhal kāfirūn
Say, "O disbelievers,

لَآ أَعْبُدُ مَا تَعْبُدُونَ ﴿٢﴾

Lā 'a'budu mā ta'budūn
I do not worship what you worship.

وَلَآ أَنتُمْ عَٰبِدُونَ مَآ أَعْبُدُ ﴿٣﴾

Wa lā 'antum 'ābidūna mā 'a'bud
Nor are you worshippers of what I worship.

وَلَآ أَنَا۠ عَابِدٌ مَّا عَبَدتُّمْ ﴿٤﴾

Wa lā 'ana 'ābidum mā 'abattum
Nor will I be a worshipper of what you worship.

وَلَآ أَنتُمْ عَـٰبِدُونَ مَآ أَعْبُدُ ﴿٥﴾

Wa lā 'antum 'ābidūna mā 'a'bud
Nor will you be worshippers of what I worship.

لَكُمْ دِينُكُمْ وَلِىَ دِينِ ﴿٦﴾

Lakum dīnukum wa liya dīn.
For you is your religion, and for me is my religion."

Juz 30 | Surah 109 | Meccan

Surah Al-Kāfirūn | The Disbelievers
6 Ayahs/Verses
TRACE AND WRITE | Word by Word

Date:_____

Part 7

7B

بِسْمِ ٱللَّهِ ٱلرَّحْمَـٰنِ ٱلرَّحِيمِ

﴿١﴾   al kāfirūna   yā 'ayyuhā   Qul

disbelievers!   O   Say,

45

Surah Al-Kāfirūn | The Disbelievers
6 Ayahs/Verses

TRACE AND TRANSLATE | Word by Word

Juz 30 | Surah 109 | Meccan

Part 7   7C

Date:_____

Translate the following:

قُلْ   يَـٰٓأَيُّهَا   ٱلْكَـٰفِرُونَ

☐ ☐ ☐

لَآ   أَعْبُدُ   مَا   تَعْبُدُونَ

☐ ☐ ☐ ☐

وَلَآ   أَنتُمْ   عَـٰبِدُونَ   مَآ   أَعْبُدُ

☐ ☐ ☐ ☐ ☐

وَلَآ   أَنَا۠   عَابِدٌ   مَّا   عَبَدتُّمْ

☐ ☐ ☐ ☐ ☐

وَلَآ   أَنتُمْ   عَـٰبِدُونَ   مَآ   أَعْبُدُ

☐ ☐ ☐ ☐ ☐

لَكُمْ   دِينُكُمْ   وَلِيَ   دِينِ

☐ ☐ ☐ ☐

Surah Al-Kāfirūn | The Disbelievers
6 Ayahs/Verses
MATCH THE PAIRS

Juz 30 | Surah 109 | Meccan

Part 7 — 7D

Date:_____

your religion	أَعْبُدُ
say	قُلْ
you are	ٱلْكَٰفِرُونَ
you worship	تَعْبُدُونَ
I worship	أَنتُمْ
disbelievers	دِينُكُمْ

Juz 30 / Surah 109 / Meccan

Surah Al-Kāfirūn | The Disbelievers
6 Ayahs/Verses

TRACE AND MEMORISE | Memorisation

Date completed: _____

Part 7 — 7E

Memorise one verse at a time.

بِسْمِ ٱللَّهِ ٱلرَّحْمَٰنِ ٱلرَّحِيمِ

﴿١﴾ قُلْ يَٰٓأَيُّهَا ٱلْكَٰفِرُونَ
Qul yā 'ayyuhal kāfirūn

﴿٢﴾ لَآ أَعْبُدُ مَا تَعْبُدُونَ
Lā 'a'budu mā ta'budūn

﴿٣﴾ وَلَآ أَنتُمْ عَٰبِدُونَ مَآ أَعْبُدُ
Wa lā 'antum 'ābidūna mā 'a'bud

﴿٤﴾ وَلَآ أَنَا عَابِدٌ مَّا عَبَدتُّمْ
Wa lā 'ana 'ābidum mā 'abattum

﴿٥﴾ وَلَآ أَنتُمْ عَٰبِدُونَ مَآ أَعْبُدُ
Wa lā 'antum 'ābidūna mā 'a'bud

﴿٦﴾ لَكُمْ دِينُكُمْ وَلِيَ دِينِ
Lakum dīnukum wa liya dīn.

Surah Al-Kawthar | Abundance
3 Ayahs/Verses
TRACE AND READ | Full Surah

Juz 30 | Surah 108 | Meccan

Part 8

بِسْمِ ٱللَّهِ ٱلرَّحْمَٰنِ ٱلرَّحِيمِ

إِنَّآ أَعْطَيْنَٰكَ ٱلْكَوْثَرَ ﴿١﴾

'Innā 'a'taynā kal kawthar
Indeed, We have granted you, [O Muḥammad], al-Kawthar.

فَصَلِّ لِرَبِّكَ وَٱنْحَرْ ﴿٢﴾

Fa ṣalli li rabbika wanḥar
So pray to your Lord and offer sacrifice [to Him alone].

إِنَّ شَانِئَكَ هُوَ ٱلْأَبْتَرُ ﴿٣﴾

'Inna shāni'aka huwal 'abtar
Indeed, your enemy is the one cut off.

Surah Al-Kawthar | Abundance
3 Ayahs/Verses

TRACE AND WRITE | Word by Word

Juz 30 | Surah 109 | Meccan

Part 8 — 8B

بِسْمِ ٱللَّهِ ٱلرَّحْمَٰنِ ٱلرَّحِيمِ

(١) إِنَّا أَعْطَيْنَاكَ ٱلْكَوْثَرَ

al kawthara	'a'taynāka	'Innā
Al Kauthar	We have given you	Indeed, We

(٢) فَصَلِّ لِرَبِّكَ وَٱنْحَرْ

wa inhar	lirabbika	Faṣalli
and sacrifice.	to your Lord	So pray

(٣) إِنَّ شَانِئَكَ هُوَ ٱلْأَبْتَرُ

al 'abtaru	huwa	shāni'aka	'Inna
the one cut off.	he (is)	your enemy	Indeed,

Surah Al-Kawthar | Abundance
3 Ayahs/Verses

TRACE AND TRANSLATE | Word by Word

Part 8 — 8C

Translate the following:

إِنَّا	أَعْطَيْنَاكَ	ٱلْكَوْثَرَ

فَصَلِّ	لِرَبِّكَ	وَٱنْحَرْ

إِنَّ	شَانِئَكَ	هُوَ	ٱلْأَبْتَرُ

Surah Al-Kawthar | Abundance
3 Ayahs/Verses
MATCH THE PAIRS

Juz 30 | Surah 108 | Meccan

Part 8 — 8D

Date:_____

he (is)	لِرَبِّكَ
indeed	هُوَ
to your Lord	إِنَّا
so pray	فَصَلِّ
and sacrifice	ٱلْكَوْثَرَ
your enemy	وَٱنْحَرْ
abundance	شَانِئَكَ

Surah Al-Kawthar | Abundance
3 Ayahs/Verses
TRACE AND MEMORISE | Memorisation

Juz 30 · Surah 108 · Meccan · Part 8 · 8E

Date completed: _____

Memorise one verse at a time.

بِسْمِ ٱللَّهِ ٱلرَّحْمَٰنِ ٱلرَّحِيمِ

(١) إِنَّا أَعْطَيْنَاكَ ٱلْكَوْثَرَ

'Innā 'a'taynā kal kawthar

(٢) فَصَلِّ لِرَبِّكَ وَٱنْحَرْ

Fa salli li rabbika wanhar

(٣) إِنَّ شَانِئَكَ هُوَ ٱلْأَبْتَرُ

'Inna shāni 'aka huwal 'abtar

Surah Al-Mā'un | Small Kindnesses
7 Ayahs/Verses

Juz 30 | Surah 107 | Meccan

TRACE AND READ | Full Surah

Date: _____

Part 9

بِسْمِ ٱللَّهِ ٱلرَّحْمَٰنِ ٱلرَّحِيمِ

أَرَءَيْتَ ٱلَّذِى يُكَذِّبُ بِٱلدِّينِ ﴿١﴾

'Ara 'aytal ladhī yu kadhdhibu biddīn
Have you seen the one who denies the Recompense?

فَذَٰلِكَ ٱلَّذِى يَدُعُّ ٱلْيَتِيمَ ﴿٢﴾

Fa dhālikal ladhi yadu'ul yatīm
For that is the one who drives away the orphan

وَلَا يَحُضُّ عَلَىٰ طَعَامِ ٱلْمِسْكِينِ ﴿٣﴾

Wa lā ya huddu'alā ta'āmil miskīn
And does not encourage the feeding of the poor.

فَوَيْلٌ لِّلْمُصَلِّينَ ﴿٤﴾

Fa way lul lil mu sallīn
So woe to those who pray

ٱلَّذِينَ هُمْ عَن صَلَاتِهِمْ سَاهُونَ ﴿٥﴾

Alladhīna hum 'an ṣalātihim sāhūn
[But] who are heedless of their prayer

ٱلَّذِينَ هُمْ يُرَآءُونَ ﴿٦﴾

Alladhīna hum yurā 'ūn
Those who make show [of their deeds]

وَيَمْنَعُونَ ٱلْمَاعُونَ ﴿٧﴾

Wa yamna'ūnal mā'ūn
And withhold [simple] assistance.

Surah Al-Mā'un | Small Kindnesses
7 Ayahs/Verses

TRACE AND WRITE | Word by Word

Part 9 — 9B

Date:_____

Juz 30 | Surah 107 | Meccan

بِسْمِ ٱللَّهِ ٱلرَّحْمَٰنِ ٱلرَّحِيمِ

(١)

| bil dīni | yukadhdhibu | alladhī | 'Ara 'ayta |

| the Judgement? | denies | the one who | Have you seen |

(٢)

| al yatīma | yadu'u | alladhī | Fadhālika |

| the orphan, | repulses | (is) the one who | Then that |

(٣)

| al miskīni | ṭa'āmi | 'alā | yaḥuḍḍu | Wa lā |

| the poor. | feed | to | feel the urge | And (does) not |

(٤)

| lilmuṣallīn | Fawaylun |

| to those who pray, | So woe |

Surah Al-Mā'un | Small Kindnesses
7 Ayahs/Verses

TRACE AND TRANSLATE | Word by Word

Translate the following:

أَرَأَيْتَ   ٱلَّذِي   يُكَذِّبُ   بِٱلدِّينِ

فَذَٰلِكَ   ٱلَّذِي   يَدُعُّ   ٱلْيَتِيمَ

وَلَا   يَحُضُّ   عَلَىٰ   طَعَامِ   ٱلْمِسْكِينِ

فَوَيْلٌ   لِّلْمُصَلِّينَ

ٱلَّذِينَ   هُمْ   عَن   صَلَاتِهِمْ   سَاهُونَ

ٱلَّذِينَ   هُمْ   يُرَاءُونَ

وَيَمْنَعُونَ   ٱلْمَاعُونَ

Surah Al-Mā'un | Small Kindnesses
7 Ayahs/Verses
MATCH THE PAIRS

Part 9

their prayers	يُكَذِّبُ
the one who	هُمْ
denies	ٱلْيَتِيمَ
the orphan	ٱلْمَاعُونَ
they	صَلَاتِهِمْ
the poor	ٱلْمِسْكِينِ
small kindness	ٱلَّذِى

Surah Al-Mā'un | Small Kindnesses
7 Ayahs/Verses

Juz 30 Surah 107 | **Meccan**

Date completed: _____

TRACE AND MEMORISE | Memorisation

Part 9 — 9E

Memorise one verse at a time.

بِسْمِ ٱللَّهِ ٱلرَّحْمَٰنِ ٱلرَّحِيمِ

{١} أَرَأَيْتَ ٱلَّذِي يُكَذِّبُ بِٱلدِّينِ
'Ara 'aytal ladhī yu kadhdhibu biddīn ✓

{٢} فَذَٰلِكَ ٱلَّذِي يَدُعُّ ٱلْيَتِيمَ
Fa dhālikal ladhi yaduʻul yatīm ✓

{٣} وَلَا يَحُضُّ عَلَىٰ طَعَامِ ٱلْمِسْكِينِ
Wa lā ya huddu ʻalā taʻāmil miskīn ✓

{٤} فَوَيْلٌ لِّلْمُصَلِّينَ
Fa way lul lil mu sallīn ✓

{٥} ٱلَّذِينَ هُمْ عَن صَلَاتِهِمْ سَاهُونَ
Alladhīna hum ʻan salātihim sāhūn ✓

{٦} ٱلَّذِينَ هُمْ يُرَآءُونَ
Alladhīna hum yurā 'ūn ✓

﴿٧﴾ وَيَمْنَعُونَ ٱلْمَاعُونَ

Wa yamna'ūnal mā'ūn

Juz 30 Surah 106	Meccan

Surah Quraysh | Quraysh
4 Ayahs/Verses
TRACE AND READ | Full Surah

Date:_____

Part 10

10A

بِسْمِ ٱللَّهِ ٱلرَّحْمَٰنِ ٱلرَّحِيمِ

لِإِيلَٰفِ قُرَيْشٍ ﴿١﴾

Li 'īlāfi quraysh
For the accustomed security of the Quraysh

إِۦلَٰفِهِمْ رِحْلَةَ ٱلشِّتَآءِ وَٱلصَّيْفِ ﴿٢﴾

'Īlāfihim rihlatash shitā'i wassayf
Their accustomed security [in] the caravan of winter and summer

فَلْيَعْبُدُوا۟ رَبَّ هَٰذَا ٱلْبَيْتِ ﴿٣﴾

Fal ya'budū rabba hādhāl bayt
Let them worship the Lord of this House,

ٱلَّذِىٓ أَطْعَمَهُم مِّن جُوعٍ وَءَامَنَهُم مِّنْ خَوْفٍۭ ﴿٤﴾

Alladhī at'amahum min jū'iw wa 'āmana hum min khawf
Who has fed them, [saving them] from hunger and made them safe, [saving them] from fear.

Surah Quraysh | Quraysh
4 Ayahs/Verses
TRACE AND WRITE | Word by Word

Juz 30 | Surah 106 | Meccan

Part 10 — 10B

Date:_____

بِسْمِ اللَّهِ الرَّحْمَٰنِ الرَّحِيمِ

{١}
qurayshin — Li ʾīlāfi
(of the) Quraysh. — For (the) familiarity

{٢}
wal sayfi — al shitāi — rihlata — ʾĪlāfihim
and summer. — (of) winter — (with the) journey — Their familiarity

{٣}
al bayti — hādhā — rabba — Falyaʿbudū
House. — (of) this — (the) Lord — So let them worship

jūʿin — min — ʾaṭʿamahum — Alladhī
(againts) hunger — [from] — feeds them — The one who

64

{٤}   خَوْفٍ   مِّنْ   وَءَامَنَهُم
         khaufin   min   wa 'āmanahum

         fear.   from   and gives them security

Juz 30 | Surah 106 | Meccan

Surah Quraysh | Quraysh
4 Ayahs/Verses
TRACE AND TRANSLATE | Word by Word

Part 10   Translate the following: **10C**

قُرَيْشٍ   لِإِيلَٰفِ

[   ]   [   ]

وَٱلصَّيْفِ   ٱلشِّتَآءِ   رِحْلَةَ   إِۦلَٰفِهِمْ

[   ]   [   ]   [   ]   [   ]

ٱلْبَيْتِ   هَٰذَا   رَبَّ   فَلْيَعْبُدُوا

[   ]   [   ]   [   ]   [   ]

جُوعٍ   مِّن   أَطْعَمَهُم   ٱلَّذِى

[   ]   [   ]   [   ]   [   ]

خَوْفٍ   مِّنْ   وَءَامَنَهُم

[   ]   [   ]   [   ]

65

Surah Quraysh | Quraysh
4 Ayahs/Verses
MATCH THE PAIRS

Juz 30 / Surah 106 / Meccan

Part 10 — 10D

Date: _____

from	رَبَّ
(the) Lord	قُرَيْشٍ
Quraysh	مِن
hunger	ٱلْبَيْتِ
and summer	ٱلشِّتَآءِ
winter	جُوعٍ
house	وَٱلصَّيْفِ

Juz 30 Surah 106 | **Meccan**

Surah Quraysh | Quraysh
4 Ayahs/Verses
TRACE AND MEMORISE | Word by Word

Date completed: _____

Part 10 **10E**

بِسْمِ اللَّهِ الرَّحْمَٰنِ الرَّحِيمِ

{١} لِإِيلَافِ قُرَيْشٍ

Li 'īlāfi quraysh ✓

{٢} إِيلَافِهِمْ رِحْلَةَ الشِّتَاءِ وَالصَّيْفِ

'Īlāfihim rihlatash shitā'i wassayf ✓

{٣} فَلْيَعْبُدُوا رَبَّ هَٰذَا الْبَيْتِ

Fal ya'budū rabba hādhāl bayt ✓

{٤} الَّذِي أَطْعَمَهُم مِّن جُوعٍ وَآمَنَهُم مِّنْ خَوْفٍ

Alladhī at'amahum min jū'iw wa 'āmana hum min khawf ✓

Surah Al-Fīl | The Elephant
5 Ayahs/Verses

Juz 30 | Surah 105 | Meccan

TRACE AND READ | Full Surah

Part 11 — 11A

بِسْمِ ٱللَّهِ ٱلرَّحْمَٰنِ ٱلرَّحِيمِ

أَلَمْ تَرَ كَيْفَ فَعَلَ رَبُّكَ بِأَصْحَٰبِ ٱلْفِيلِ ﴿١﴾

'Alam tara kayfa fa'ala rabbuka bi aṣ ḥābil fīl

Have you not considered, [O Muḥammad], how your Lord dealt with the companions of the elephant?

أَلَمْ يَجْعَلْ كَيْدَهُمْ فِي تَضْلِيلٍ ﴿٢﴾

'Alam yaj'al kay dahum fī taḍ līl

Did He not make their plan into misguidance?

وَأَرْسَلَ عَلَيْهِمْ طَيْرًا أَبَابِيلَ ﴿٣﴾

Wa 'arsala 'alayhim ṭayran 'abābīl

And He sent against them birds in flocks,

تَرْمِيهِم بِحِجَارَةٍ مِّن سِجِّيلٍ ﴿٤﴾

Tar mīhim bi ḥi jāratim min sijjīl

Striking them with stones of hard clay,

فَجَعَلَهُمْ كَعَصْفٍ مَّأْكُولٍ ﴿٥﴾

Faja 'alahum ka'asfim ma'kūl

And He made them like eaten straw.

Juz 30 | Surah 105 | Meccan

Surah Al-Fīl | The Elephant
5 Ayahs/Verses

TRACE AND WRITE | Word by Word

Date:_____

Part 11 — 11B

بِسْمِ ٱللَّهِ ٱلرَّحْمَٰنِ ٱلرَّحِيمِ

'Alam	tara	kayfa	fa'ala
Have not	you seen	how	dealt

(1)

rabbuka	bi 'aṣḥābi	al fīli
your Lord	(with the) Companions	(of) the Elephant?

(2)

'Alam	yaj'al	kaydahum	fī	tadlīlin
Did not	He make	their plan	go	astray?

69

﴿٣﴾ وَأَرْسَلَ عَلَيْهِمْ طَيْرًا أَبَابِيلَ

Wa 'arsala   'alayhim   tayran   'abābīla

And He sent   against them   birds   (in) flocks.

﴿٤﴾ تَرْمِيهِم بِحِجَارَةٍ مِّن سِجِّيلٍ

Tarmīhim   bihijāratin   min   sijjīlin

Striking them   with stones   of   baked tray.

﴿٥﴾ فَجَعَلَهُمْ كَعَصْفٍ مَّأْكُولٍ

Faja'alahum   ka'asfin   ma'kūlin

Then He made them   like straw   eaten up.

Surah Al-Fīl | The Elephant
5 Ayahs/Verses
TRACE AND TRANSLATE | Word by Word

Juz 30 · Surah 105 · Meccan · Part 11 · 11C

Translate the following:

أَلَمْ   تَرَ   كَيْفَ   فَعَلَ

رَبُّكَ   بِأَصْحَابِ   الْفِيلِ

أَلَمْ   يَجْعَلْ   كَيْدَهُمْ   فِي تَضْلِيلٍ

وَأَرْسَلَ   عَلَيْهِمْ   طَيْرًا   أَبَابِيلَ

تَرْمِيهِمْ   بِحِجَارَةٍ   مِنْ   سِجِّيلٍ

فَجَعَلَهُمْ   كَعَصْفٍ   مَأْكُولٍ

Surah Al-Fīl | The Elephant
5 Ayahs/Verses
MATCH THE PAIRS

Juz 30 / Surah 105 / Meccan

Part 11 — 11D

birds	ٱلْفِيلِ
their plan	رَبُّكَ
the elephants	طَيْرًا
how	أَبَابِيلَ
your Lord	كَيْدَهُمْ
(in) flocks	كَيْفَ

Surah Al-Fīl | The Elephant
5 Ayahs/Verses

Juz 30 · Surah 105 · Meccan

Part 11 — **11E**

TRACE AND MEMORISE | Memorisation

Date completed: _____

Memorise one verse at a time.

بِسْمِ ٱللَّهِ ٱلرَّحْمَٰنِ ٱلرَّحِيمِ

﴿١﴾ أَلَمْ تَرَ كَيْفَ فَعَلَ رَبُّكَ بِأَصْحَٰبِ ٱلْفِيلِ
'Alam tara kayfa fa'ala rabbuka bi aṣ ḥābil fīl

﴿٢﴾ أَلَمْ يَجْعَلْ كَيْدَهُمْ فِى تَضْلِيلٍ
'Alam yaj'al kay dahum fī taḍ līl

﴿٣﴾ وَأَرْسَلَ عَلَيْهِمْ طَيْرًا أَبَابِيلَ
Wa 'arsala 'alayhim tayran 'abābīl

﴿٤﴾ تَرْمِيهِم بِحِجَارَةٍ مِّن سِجِّيلٍ
Tar mīhim bi hi jāratim min sij jīl

﴿٥﴾ فَجَعَلَهُمْ كَعَصْفٍ مَّأْكُولٍ
Faja 'alahum ka'aṣfim ma'kūl

73

Surah Al-Humazah | The Traducer
9 Ayahs/Verses
TRACE AND READ | Full Surah

Juz 30 | Surah 104 | Meccan

Part 12 — 12A

بِسْمِ ٱللَّهِ ٱلرَّحْمَٰنِ ٱلرَّحِيمِ

وَيْلٌ لِّكُلِّ هُمَزَةٍ لُّمَزَةٍ ﴿١﴾

Way lullikulli humazatillumazah
Woe to every scorner and mocker

ٱلَّذِى جَمَعَ مَالًا وَعَدَّدَهُۥ ﴿٢﴾

Alladhī jama'a mālaw wa'addadah
Who collects wealth and [continuously] counts it.

يَحْسَبُ أَنَّ مَالَهُۥٓ أَخْلَدَهُۥ ﴿٣﴾

Yahsabu'anna mālahū akhladah
He thinks that his wealth will make him immortal.

كَلَّا ۖ لَيُنۢبَذَنَّ فِى ٱلْحُطَمَةِ ﴿٤﴾

Kallā layumbadhanna fīlhutamah
No! He will surely be thrown into the Crusher.

74

وَمَآ أَدْرَىٰكَ مَا ٱلْحُطَمَةُ ﴿٥﴾

Wa mā 'adrāka malhutamah
And what can make you know what is the Crusher?

نَارُ ٱللَّهِ ٱلْمُوقَدَةُ ﴿٦﴾

Nārullāhilmūqadah
It is the fire of Allāh, [eternally] fueled,

ٱلَّتِى تَطَّلِعُ عَلَى ٱلْأَفْـِٔدَةِ ﴿٧﴾

Al latī tattali'u 'alal 'af'idah
Which mounts directed at the hearts.

إِنَّهَا عَلَيْهِم مُّؤْصَدَةٌ ﴿٨﴾

'Innahā 'alayhim mu'sadah
Indeed, it [i.e., Hellfire] will be closed down upon them

فِى عَمَدٍ مُّمَدَّدَةٍ ﴿٩﴾

Fī 'amadim mumaddadah
In extended columns.

Surah Al-Humazah | The Traducer
9 Ayahs/Verses
TRACE AND WRITE | Word by Word

Juz 30 | Surah 104 | Meccan

Part 12 | 12B

بِسْمِ ٱللَّهِ ٱلرَّحْمَٰنِ ٱلرَّحِيمِ

{1} lumazatin — humazatin — likulli — Waylun

backbiter! — slanderer — to every — Woe

{2} wa 'addadahū — mālan — jama'a — Alladhī

and counts it. — wealth — collects — The one who

{3} 'akhladahū — mālahū — 'anna — Yaḥsabu

will make him immortal. — his wealth — that — Thinking

{4} al ḥuṭamati — fī — layunbadhanna — Kallā

the Crusher. — in — Surely he will be thrown — Nay!

76

{5} وَمَا أَدْرَاكَ مَا ٱلْحُطَمَةُ

al hutamatu mā 'adrāka Wamā

the Crusher (is)? what will make you know And what

{6} نَارُ ٱللَّهِ ٱلْمُوقَدَةُ

al mūqadatu al lahi Nāru

A fire Allāh kindled.

{7} ٱلَّتِي تَطَّلِعُ عَلَى ٱلْأَفْئِدَةِ

al 'af'idati 'alā tattali'u Allatī

Which mounts up to the hearts.

{8} إِنَّهَا عَلَيْهِم مُّؤْصَدَةٌ

mu'sadatun 'alayhim 'Innahā

Indeed, it (will be) upon them closed over.

{9} فِي عَمَدٍ مُّمَدَّدَةٍ

mumaddadatin 'amadin Fī

In columns extended.

Surah Al-Humazah | The Traducer
9 Ayahs/Verses

Juz 30 / Surah 104 / Meccan

Part 12 — **12C**

Date:_____

TRACE AND TRANSLATE | Word by Word

Translate the following:

لُمَزَةٍ	هُمَزَةٍ	لِّكُلِّ	وَيْلٌ

وَعَدَّدَهُ	مَالًا	جَمَعَ	ٱلَّذِي

أَخْلَدَهُ	مَالَهُ	أَنَّ	يَحْسَبُ

ٱلْحُطَمَةِ	فِي	لَيُنۢبَذَنَّ	كَلَّا

ٱلْحُطَمَةُ	مَا	أَدْرَىٰكَ	وَمَا

ٱلْمُوقَدَةُ	ٱللَّهِ	نَارُ

ٱلْأَفْـِٔدَةِ	عَلَى	تَطَّلِعُ	ٱلَّتِي

إِنَّهَا   عَلَيْهِم   مُوصَدَةٌ

فِي   عَمَدٍ   مُمَدَّدَةٍ

Surah Al-Humazah | The Traducer
9 Ayahs/Verses
MATCH THE PAIRS

Juz 30 | Surah 104 | Meccan

Part 12 — 12D

the Crusher	جَمَعَ
the one who	ٱلَّذِى
collects	هُمَزَةٍ
a fire	ٱلْحُطَمَةِ
backbiter	نَارُ
the hearts	ٱلْأَفْئِدَةِ
slanderer	لُّمَزَةٍ

Surah Al-Humazah | The Traducer
9 Ayahs/Verses
TRACE AND MEMORISE | Memorisation

Juz 30 | Surah 104 | Meccan

Part 12 — 12E

Date completed: _____

Memorise one verse at a time.

بِسْمِ ٱللَّهِ ٱلرَّحْمَٰنِ ٱلرَّحِيمِ

{١} وَيْلٌ لِّكُلِّ هُمَزَةٍ لُّمَزَةٍ
Way lullikulli humazatillumazah ✓

{٢} ٱلَّذِي جَمَعَ مَالًا وَعَدَّدَهُ
Alladhī jama'a mālaw wa'addadah ✓

{٣} يَحْسَبُ أَنَّ مَالَهُ أَخْلَدَهُ
Yahsabu 'anna mālahū akhladah ✓

{٤} كَلَّا ۖ لَيُنبَذَنَّ فِي ٱلْحُطَمَةِ
Kallā layumbadhanna fīlhutamah ✓

{٥} وَمَا أَدْرَاكَ مَا ٱلْحُطَمَةُ
Wa mā 'adrāka malhutamah ✓

{٦} نَارُ ٱللَّهِ ٱلْمُوقَدَةُ
Nārullāhilmūqadah

81

{٧} اَلَّتِي تَطَّلِعُ عَلَى ٱلْأَفْئِدَةِ
Allatī tattaliʻu ʻalal ʼafʼidah

{٨} إِنَّهَا عَلَيْهِم مُّؤْصَدَةٌ
ʼInnahā ʻalayhim muʼṣadah

{٩} فِي عَمَدٍ مُّمَدَّدَةٍ
Fī ʻamadim mumaddadah

| Juz 30 Surah 103 | Meccan |

Surah Al-'Asr | The Declining Day
3 Ayahs/Verses
TRACE AND READ | Full Surah

Date:_____

Part 13

13A

بِسْمِ ٱللَّهِ ٱلرَّحْمَٰنِ ٱلرَّحِيمِ

وَٱلْعَصْرِ ﴿١﴾

Wal 'asr
By time

إِنَّ ٱلْإِنسَٰنَ لَفِى خُسْرٍ ﴿٢﴾

'Innal 'insāna lafī khusr
Indeed, mankind is in loss,

إِلَّا ٱلَّذِينَ ءَامَنُوا۟ وَعَمِلُوا۟ ٱلصَّٰلِحَٰتِ

'Illalladhīna 'āmanu wa'amilussālihāti
Except for those who have believed and done righteous deeds

وَتَوَاصَوْا۟ بِٱلْحَقِّ وَتَوَاصَوْا۟ بِٱلصَّبْرِ ﴿٣﴾

wa tawā saw bilhaqqi wa tawā sawbissabr
and advised each other to truth and advised each other to patience.

Surah Al-'Asr | The Declining Day
3 Ayahs/Verses
TRACE AND WRITE | Word by Word

Part 13 — 13B

بِسْمِ اللَّهِ الرَّحْمَٰنِ الرَّحِيمِ

{1} Wal'asri — By the time,

{2} khusrin — lafī — al 'insāna — 'Inna
loss, — (is) surely in — mankind — Indeed,

al sāliḥāti — wa 'amilū — 'āmanū — alladhīna — 'Illā
righteous deeds — and do — believe — those who — Except

{3} bil ṣabri — watawāṣaw — bil ḥaqqi — watawāṣaw
to (the) patience. — and enjoin (each other) — to the truth — and enjoin (each other)

Surah Al-'Asr | The Declining Day
3 Ayahs/Verses

TRACE AND TRANSLATE | Word by Word

Juz 30 | Surah 103 | Meccan

Part 13 | 13C

Date:_____

Translate the following:

وَٱلْعَصْرِ

إِنَّ ٱلْإِنسَٰنَ لَفِى خُسْرٍ

إِلَّا ٱلَّذِينَ ءَامَنُوا۟ وَعَمِلُوا۟ ٱلصَّٰلِحَٰتِ

وَتَوَاصَوْا۟ بِٱلْحَقِّ وَتَوَاصَوْا۟ بِٱلصَّبْرِ

Surah Al-'Asr | The Declining Day
3 Ayahs/Verses

Juz 30 | Surah 103 | Meccan

Part 13 — 13D

MATCH THE PAIRS

Date: _____

to (the) patience	ٱلصَّٰلِحَٰتِ
those who	وَٱلْعَصْرِ
indeed	ٱلَّذِينَ
believe	بِٱلصَّبْرِ
to the truth	بِٱلْحَقِّ
righteous deeds	ءَامَنُوا
by the time	إِنَّ

Surah Al-'Asr | The Declining Day
3 Ayahs/Verses

Juz 30 | Surah 103 | Meccan | Part 13 | 13E

Date completed: _____

TRACE AND MEMORISE | Memorisation

Memorise one verse at a time.

بِسْمِ ٱللَّهِ ٱلرَّحْمَٰنِ ٱلرَّحِيمِ

(١) وَٱلْعَصْرِ
Wal 'asr ✓

(٢) إِنَّ ٱلْإِنسَٰنَ لَفِى خُسْرٍ
'Innal 'insāna lafī khusr ✓

إِلَّا ٱلَّذِينَ ءَامَنُوا۟ وَعَمِلُوا۟ ٱلصَّٰلِحَٰتِ
'Illalladhīna 'āmanu wa'amilussālihāti ✓

(٣) وَتَوَاصَوْا۟ بِٱلْحَقِّ وَتَوَاصَوْا۟ بِٱلصَّبْرِ
wa tawā saw bilhaqqi wa tawā sawbissabr

87

Juz 30 | Surah 102 | Meccan

Surah At-Takāthur | Competition
8 Ayahs/Verses
TRACE AND READ | Full Surah

Date:_____

Part 14 — 14A

بِسْمِ ٱللَّهِ ٱلرَّحْمَٰنِ ٱلرَّحِيمِ

أَلْهَىٰكُمُ ٱلتَّكَاثُرُ ﴿١﴾

'Al hākumut takāthur
Competition in [worldly] increase diverts you

حَتَّىٰ زُرْتُمُ ٱلْمَقَابِرَ ﴿٢﴾

Hattā zurtumul maqābir
Until you visit the graveyards.

كَلَّا سَوْفَ تَعْلَمُونَ ﴿٣﴾

Kallā sawfa ta'lamūn
No! You are going to know.

ثُمَّ كَلَّا سَوْفَ تَعْلَمُونَ ﴿٤﴾

Thumma kallā sawfa ta'lamūn
Then, no! You are going to know.

كَلَّا لَوْ تَعْلَمُونَ عِلْمَ ٱلْيَقِينِ ﴿٥﴾

Kallā law ta'lamūna 'ilmal yaqīn

No! If you only knew with knowledge of certainty...

لَتَرَوُنَّ ٱلْجَحِيمَ ﴿٦﴾

Latarawunnal ja<u>h</u>īm

You will surely see the Hellfire.

ثُمَّ لَتَرَوُنَّهَا عَيْنَ ٱلْيَقِينِ ﴿٧﴾

Thumma latarawunnahā 'aynal yaqīn

Then you will surely see it with the eye of certainty.

ثُمَّ لَتُسْـَٔلُنَّ يَوْمَئِذٍ عَنِ ٱلنَّعِيمِ ﴿٨﴾

Thumma latus'alunna yawma'idhin 'anin na'īm

Then you will surely be asked that Day about pleasure.

Surah At-Takāthur | Competition
8 Ayahs/Verses

Juz 30 | Surah 102 | Meccan

TRACE AND WRITE | Word by Word

Part 14 — 14B

Date:_____

بِسْمِ اللَّهِ الرَّحْمَٰنِ الرَّحِيمِ

{1} al takāthuru / 'Alhākumu
the competition to increase / Diverts you

{2} al maqābira / zurtumu / Hattā
the graves. / you visit / Until

{3} ta'lamūna / sawfa / Kallā
you will know. / Soon / Nay!

{4} ta'lamūna / sawfa / kallā / Thumma
you will know. / Soon / nay! / Then.

90

Surah At-Takāthur | Competition
8 Ayahs/Verses
TRACE AND TRANSLATE | Word by Word

Juz 30 / Surah 102 / Meccan

Part 14 — **14C**

Date:_____

Translate the following:

ٱلتَّكَاثُرُ   أَلْهَىٰكُمُ

ٱلْمَقَابِرَ   زُرْتُمُ   حَتَّىٰ

تَعْلَمُونَ   سَوْفَ   كَلَّا

تَعْلَمُونَ   سَوْفَ   كَلَّا   ثُمَّ

ٱلْيَقِينِ   عِلْمَ   تَعْلَمُونَ   لَوْ   كَلَّا

ٱلْجَحِيمَ   لَتَرَوُنَّ

ٱلْيَقِينِ   عَيْنَ   لَتَرَوُنَّهَا   ثُمَّ

ٱلنَّعِيمِ   عَنِ   يَوْمَئِذٍ   لَتُسْأَلُنَّ   ثُمَّ

Surah At-Takāthur | Competition
8 Ayahs/Verses
MATCH THE PAIRS

Juz 30 Surah 102 — Meccan

Part 14 — 14D

the pleasures	عِلْمَ
certainty	سَوْفَ
the Hellfire	ٱلنَّعِيمِ
soon	ٱلْيَقِينِ
that day	ٱلْجَحِيمَ
the graves	يَوْمَئِذٍ
knowledge	ٱلْمَقَابِرَ

Surah At-Takāthur | Competition
8 Ayahs/Verses
TRACE AND MEMORISE | Memorisation

Juz 30 | Surah 102 | Meccan

Date completed: _____

Part 14 — 14E

Memorise one verse at a time.

بِسْمِ اللَّهِ الرَّحْمَٰنِ الرَّحِيمِ

(١) أَلْهَاكُمُ التَّكَاثُرُ
'Al hākumut takāthur

(٢) حَتَّىٰ زُرْتُمُ الْمَقَابِرَ
Hattā zurtumul maqābir

(٣) كَلَّا سَوْفَ تَعْلَمُونَ
Kallā sawfa ta'lamūn

(٤) ثُمَّ كَلَّا سَوْفَ تَعْلَمُونَ
Thumma kallā sawfa ta'lamūn

(٥) كَلَّا لَوْ تَعْلَمُونَ عِلْمَ الْيَقِينِ
Kallā law ta'lamūna 'ilmal yaqīn

(٦) لَتَرَوُنَّ الْجَحِيمَ
Latarawunnal jahīm

﴿٧﴾ ثُمَّ لَتَرَوُنَّهَا عَيْنَ ٱلْيَقِينِ

Thumma latarawunnahā 'aynal yaqīn ✓

﴿٨﴾ ثُمَّ لَتُسْأَلُنَّ يَوْمَئِذٍ عَنِ ٱلنَّعِيمِ

Thumma latus'alunna yawma 'idhin 'anin na'īm ✓

Ayatul Kursi | the Throne Verse
Ayah/Verse No: 255

Juz 1 Part of Surah 2 | **Medinan**

Date: _____

TRACE AND READ | Full Ayah

Part 15 — 15A

verse no: 255

اللَّهُ لَا إِلَٰهَ إِلَّا هُوَ الْحَيُّ الْقَيُّومُ ﴿٢٥٥﴾

Allāhu lā ilāha illā huwal ḥayyul qayyūm
Allah - there is no deity except Him, the Ever-Living, the Self-Sustaining.

لَا تَأْخُذُهُ سِنَةٌ وَلَا نَوْمٌ

lā ta' khudhuhū sinatu wa lā nawm
Neither drowsiness overtakes Him nor sleep.

لَهُۥ مَا فِي السَّمَٰوَٰتِ وَمَا فِي الْأَرْضِ

lahū mā fissamāwāti wa mā fīl ard
To Him belongs whatever is in the heavens and whatever is on the earth.

مَن ذَا الَّذِى يَشْفَعُ عِندَهُۥ إِلَّا بِإِذْنِهِۦ

man dhā lladhī yashfa'u 'indahū illā bi idhnih
Who is it that can intercede with Him except by His permission?

يَعْلَمُ مَا بَيْنَ أَيْدِيهِمْ وَمَا خَلْفَهُمْ

ya' lamu mā bayna aydīhim wa mā khalfahum

He knows what is [presently] before them and what will be after them,

وَلَا يُحِيطُونَ بِشَيْءٍ مِّنْ عِلْمِهِ إِلَّا بِمَا شَآءَ

wa lā yu ḥīṭūna bi shay-i mmin 'ilmihī illā bi mā shāa'

and they encompass not a thing of His knowledge except for what He wills.

وَسِعَ كُرْسِيُّهُ ٱلسَّمَٰوَٰتِ وَٱلْأَرْضَ

wasi'a kursiyyuhus samāwāti wal ard

His Kursī extends over the heavens and the earth,

وَلَا يَئُودُهُ حِفْظُهُمَا وَهُوَ ٱلْعَلِيُّ ٱلْعَظِيمُ

wa lā yaūduhū ḥifdhuhumā wa huwal 'aliyyul 'adhīm

and their preservation tires Him not. And He is the Most High, the Most Great.

Ayatul Kursi | the Throne Verse
Ayah/Verse No: 255
TRACE AND WRITE | Word by Word

Juz 1 Part of Surah 2 | Medinan

Part 15 — 15B

{ ٢٥٥ }

| al-qayyūmu | al-hayyu | huwa | illā | ilāha | lā | Al lāhu |
| the Sustainer of all that exists | the Ever-Living | Him | except | God | (there is) no | Allah |

| nawmun | walā | sinatun | ta'khudhuhū | lā |
| sleep | (and) not | slumber | overtakes Him | not |

| al ardi | fī | wa mā | al samāwāti | fī | mā | lahū |
| the earth | (is) in | and what(ever) | the heavens | (is) in | what(ever) | to Him (belongs) |

| bi idhnihi | illā | 'indahū | yashfa'u | alladhī | dhā | man |
| by His permission | except | with Him | can intercede | who | (is) the one | who |

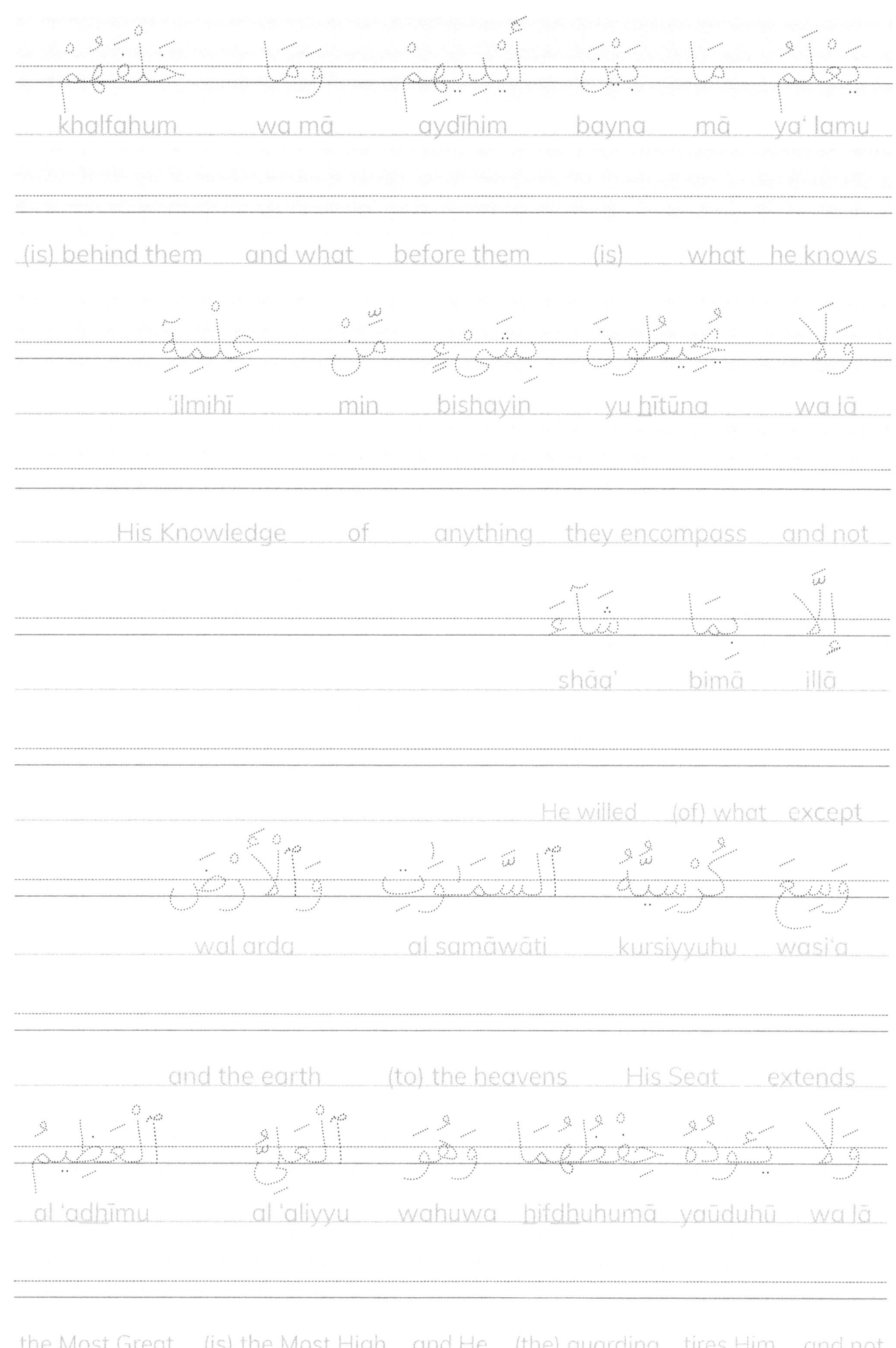

Ayatul Kursi | the Throne Verse
Ayah/Verse No: 255

TRACE AND TRANSLATE | Word by Word

Translate the following:

اللَّهُ لَا إِلَٰهَ إِلَّا هُوَ الْحَيُّ الْقَيُّومُ

لَا تَأْخُذُهُ سِنَةٌ وَلَا نَوْمٌ

لَهُ مَا فِي السَّمَاوَاتِ وَمَا فِي الْأَرْضِ

مَن ذَا الَّذِي يَشْفَعُ عِندَهُ إِلَّا بِإِذْنِهِ

يَعْلَمُ مَا بَيْنَ أَيْدِيهِمْ وَمَا خَلْفَهُمْ

وَلَا يُحِيطُونَ بِشَيْءٍ مِّنْ عِلْمِهِ إِلَّا بِمَا شَاءَ

وَسِعَ كُرْسِيُّهُ السَّمَاوَاتِ وَالْأَرْضَ

وَلَا يَئُودُهُ حِفْظُهُمَا وَهُوَ الْعَلِيُّ الْعَظِيمُ

Ayatul Kursi | the Throne Verse
Ayah/Verse No: 255

MATCH THE PAIRS

His Seat	نَوْمٌ
the heavens	ٱلْأَرْضِ
the earth	ٱلْعَلِيُّ
sleep	مَن
the Most High	كُرْسِيُّهُ
who	ٱلْحَيُّ
the Ever Living	ٱلسَّمَٰوَٰتِ

Ayatul Kursi | the Throne Verse
Ayah/Verse No: 255

TRACE AND MEMORISE | Memorisation

Juz 1 Part of Surah 2 — Medinan

Part 15

Date completed: _____

Memorise one verse at a time.

بِسْمِ اللَّهِ الرَّحْمَٰنِ الرَّحِيمِ

{٢٥٥} اللَّهُ لَا إِلَٰهَ إِلَّا هُوَ الْحَيُّ الْقَيُّومُ

Allāhu lā ilāha illā huwal hayyul qayyūm

لَا تَأْخُذُهُ سِنَةٌ وَلَا نَوْمٌ

lā ta' khudhuhū sinatu wa lā nawm

لَهُ مَا فِي السَّمَاوَاتِ وَمَا فِي الْأَرْضِ

lahū mā fīs-samāwāti wa mā fīl ard

مَن ذَا الَّذِي يَشْفَعُ عِنْدَهُ إِلَّا بِإِذْنِهِ

man dhā lladhī yashfa'u 'indahū illā bi idhnih

يَعْلَمُ مَا بَيْنَ أَيْدِيهِمْ وَمَا خَلْفَهُمْ

ya' lamu mā bayna aydīhim wa mā khalfahum

وَلَا يُحِيطُونَ بِشَيْءٍ مِّنْ عِلْمِهِ إِلَّا بِمَا شَاءَ

wa lā yu hītūna bi shay-i mmin 'ilmihī illā bi mā shāa'

وَسِعَ كُرْسِيُّهُ ٱلسَّمَٰوَٰتِ وَٱلْأَرْضَ

wasi'a kursiyyuhus samāwāti wal ard

✓

وَلَا يَـُٔودُهُۥ حِفْظُهُمَا وَهُوَ ٱلْعَلِيُّ ٱلْعَظِيمُ

wa lā yaūduhū hifdhuhumā wa huwal 'aliyyul 'adhīm

✓

MY SURAH TRACKER

Colour in the star when you've memorised the whole surah.

Surah Al-Fatihah ☆	Surah An-Nās ☆	Surah Al-Falaq ☆	Surah Al-Ikhlās ☆
Date completed: _____	Date completed: _____	Date completed: _____	Date completed: _____

Surah Al-Masad 	Surah An-Nasr 	Surah Al-Kāfirūn 	Surah Al-Kawthar ☆
Date completed: _____	Date completed: _____	Date completed: _____	Date completed: _____

Surah Al-Māʻun 	Surah Quraysh 	Surah Al-Fil	Surah Al-Humazah 
Date completed: _____	Date completed: _____	Date completed: _____	Date completed: _____

Surah Al-Asr 	Surah At-Takāthur 	Ayatul Kursi 
Date completed: _____	Date completed: _____	Date completed: _____

www.ingramcontent.com/pod-product-compliance
Lightning Source LLC
Chambersburg PA
CBHW041625020526
44119CB00058BA/845